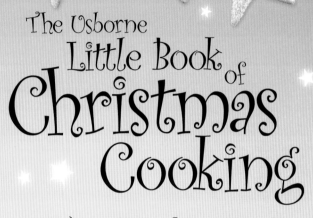

The Usborne
Little Book of
Christmas
Cooking

Rebecca Gilpin, Leonie Pratt
and Catherine Atkinson

Designed by Josephine Thompson,
Non Figg, Amanda Gulliver,
Katrina Fearn and Doriana Berkovic

Illustrated by Kim Lane, Sue Stitt,
Molly Sage and Non Figg

Photographs by Howard Allman

Contents

Some of these biscuits are decorated with sparkly writing icing, as well as white icing.

Snowflake biscuits

To make about 14 biscuits, you will need:

75g (3oz) butter, softened
25g (1oz) icing sugar
115g (4oz) plain flour
white writing icing
a round cutter, about 6cm (2½in)

Before you start, wipe cooking oil over two baking trays.
You will need to heat your oven to 180°C, 350°F, gas mark 4 in step 3.

❄ Keep the biscuits in an airtight container and eat them within five days.

1. Put the butter into a large bowl. Stir it until it is creamy. Sift the icing sugar into the bowl and stir it in, until the mixture is smooth.

2. Sift the flour into the bowl and stir it in with a wooden spoon. Then, using your hands, squeeze the mixture to make a dough.

Flatten the dough a little before you wrap it.

3. Wrap the dough in plastic foodwrap and put it in a fridge for 30 minutes. While the dough chills, turn on your oven.

4

Try drawing different patterns on some of the biscuits.

4. Dust a rolling pin and a clean work surface with flour. Roll out the dough until it is slightly thinner than your little finger.

5. Cut out lots of circles with the cutter. Then, squeeze the scraps into a ball and roll it out. Cut out more circles.

6. When you have used all the dough, put the circles onto the baking trays. Then, bake the biscuits for 10-12 minutes.

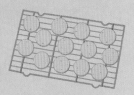

7. Leave the biscuits on the baking trays for two minutes. Then, move them onto a wire rack with a spatula and let them cool.

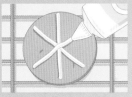

8. Draw a line down the middle of one biscuit with white writing icing. Draw two more lines crossing over the first one, like this.

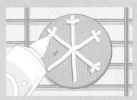

9. Make a snowflake by adding small lines of writing icing across the ends of the lines. Then, decorate all the other biscuits, too.

Pretty pear pies

To make 12 pies, you will need:

375g (13oz) shortcrust pastry, taken out
  of the fridge 20 minutes before you start.
1 small orange
15g (½oz) butter
25g (1oz) soft light brown sugar
25g (1oz) dried cranberries
half a teaspoon of ground cinnamon
2 soft, sweet pears or four pear halves from a tin

milk for glazing
icing sugar for dusting
a 12-hole baking tray
a 7.5cm (3in) round cutter
  and a star-shaped cutter

Before you start, wipe cooking oil in the holes in the baking tray.
Heat your oven to 190°C, 375°F, gas mark 5 in step 5.

❄ Keep the pies in an airtight container and eat them within five days.

You don't need the other half
of the orange.

1. Grate half the rind from
the orange using the fine
holes on a grater. Cut the
orange in half and squeeze
the juice from one half.

2. Put the rind and one
tablespoon of the orange
juice into a pan. Then, add
the butter, brown sugar,
cranberries and cinnamon.

3. Carefully peel the pears
with a vegetable peeler. Cut
them into quarters and cut
out the cores. Then, cut the
quarters into small pieces.

Keep stirring the mixture
so that it doesn't stick.

Dust the
rolling pin
with flour,
too.

Cut the circles as
close together
as you can.

4. Put the pieces of pear
into the pan. Gently heat
the mixture on a low heat
for 10 minutes. Take it off
the heat and let it cool.

5. Turn on your oven. Dust
a clean work surface with
flour and roll out the pastry
until it is slightly thinner
than your little finger.

6. Cut 12 circles from the
pastry with the round
cutter. Then, press the
scraps together to make
a ball and put it to one side.

The milk will make the pastry shiny when it is cooked.

The pies can be eaten warm or cold.

7. Press the circles into the pans in the baking tray. Then, put a heaped teaspoon of the pear mixture into each one.

8. Roll out the ball of pastry and cut out 12 stars with the star cutter. Lay the stars on the pies, then brush milk over them.

Wear oven gloves.

9. Bake the pies for 20 minutes, until they are golden. Then, lift them out and leave them in the tray to cool for 10 minutes.

10. Using a blunt knife, lift the pies onto a plate. Put a little icing sugar into a sieve and sprinkle the sugar over the pies.

You could serve the pies with a spoonful of crème fraîche.

Christmas fairy crowns

To make 16 biscuits,
you will need:

50g (2oz) butter
3 tablespoons golden syrup
175g (6oz) self-raising flour
half a teaspoon of ground cinnamon
half a teaspoon of bicarbonate
 of soda
1 tablespoon of light soft brown
 sugar
2 tablespoons milk
writing icing and sweets for
 decorating

Before you start, wipe cooking
oil over two baking trays.
Heat your oven to 180°C,
350°F, gas mark 4 in step 5.

❋ Keep the biscuits in an airtight
 container and eat them within
 three days.

1. Cut the butter into
cubes and put them into
a small pan. Add the
golden syrup, then gently
heat the pan on a low heat.

2. Stir the mixture every
now and then, until it has
just melted. Then, take the
pan off the heat and let it
cool for three minutes.

3. Sift the flour, cinnamon
and bicarbonate of soda
into a bowl and stir in the
brown sugar. Make a hollow
in the middle with a spoon.

4. Carefully pour the butter
and syrup mixture into the
hollow. Add the milk and
stir everything until you
have made a dough.

Flatten the dough a little
before you wrap it.

5. Wrap the dough in
plastic foodwrap and put
it in the fridge for 15
minutes. While the dough is
chilling, turn on your oven.

You could use different colours of writing icing to draw patterns on your crowns.

Roll out the dough slowly but firmly.

6. Dust a rolling pin and a clean work surface with some flour. Roll out the dough until it is half as thick as your little finger.

7. Cut off the wobbly edges of the dough with a sharp knife, to make a square. Then, cut the square into four pieces, like this.

8. Cut each piece in half, to make a rectangle. Then, make each rectangle into a crown by cutting out two small triangles at the top.

Use a spatula.

9. Squeeze the scraps into a ball and roll it out. Cut out more crowns, then put all of the crowns onto the baking trays.

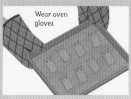

Wear oven gloves.

10. Bake the crowns for 8-10 minutes. Carefully lift them out of the oven and leave them on the baking trays for five minutes.

Stick on sweets with dots of icing.

11. Lift the crowns onto a wire rack with a spatula, and let them cool. Then, decorate them with writing icing and sweets for jewels.

Shining star biscuits

To make about 20 biscuits, you will need:

50g (2oz) light soft brown sugar
50g (2oz) butter, softened
a small egg
115g (4½oz) plain flour
15g (½oz) cornflour
1 teaspoon of ground mixed spice
solid boiled sweets

a large star-shaped cutter
a fat drinking straw
a small round cutter, slightly
  bigger than the sweets

Heat the oven to 180°C, 350°F, gas mark 4, before you start.

❄ The biscuits need to be kept in an airtight
  container and eaten within three days.

Thread thin ribbon
through the holes.

1. Put the sugar and butter into a large bowl. Stir them together with a wooden spoon, until the mixture is smooth.

2. Break the egg into a separate bowl. Use a fork to stir the egg hard, until the yolk and the white are mixed together.

3. Mix half of the beaten egg into the mixture in the bowl, a little at a time. You don't need the other half of the egg mixture.

4. Sift the flour, cornflour and mixed spice into the bowl. Then, use a wooden spoon to mix everything together really well.

5. Use your hands to squeeze the mixture together to make a dough. Then, squeeze the dough into a large ball.

6. Dust a clean work surface and a rolling pin with flour. Roll out the ball of dough until it is a little thinner than your little finger.

Don't eat the biscuits if you hang them on a Christmas tree.

Use a spatula.

7. Draw around a baking tray on baking parchment. Cut out the rectangle and put it in the tray. Then, cut out stars from the dough.

8. Make a hole in each star by pressing the drinking straw through the dough, near to the top of one of the points.

9. Use the small round cutter to cut a hole in the middle of each star. The hole should be slightly bigger than a boiled sweet.

10. Squeeze the scraps into a ball. Then, roll it out and cut more stars. Put them on the baking tray and make holes in them.

11. Put a sweet into the middle of each star. Put the baking tray on the middle shelf of the oven and bake the stars for 12 minutes.

12. Wearing oven gloves, take the biscuits out of the oven. Leave them on the baking tray until they have cooled.

Festive fruit cups

To make 12 festive fruit cups, you will need:

50g (2oz) sweetened dried pineapple
or mango
1 tablespoon of pineapple or orange juice
100g (4oz) milk chocolate drops
100g (4oz) white chocolate drops
small foil or double thickness paper cases

❋ Keep the fruit cups in an airtight container
and eat them within five days.

1. Put the pineapple or mango onto a chopping board. Then, using a sharp knife, carefully cut the fruit into tiny pieces.

2. Put about a quarter of the chopped fruit to one side. Put the rest into a small bowl, and add the fruit juice. Stir it well.

3. Cover the bowl with plastic foodwrap. Then, leave the fruit for half an hour or until it has soaked up the juice.

Do this while the fruit is soaking.

Wear oven gloves when you lift the bowl out.

4. Fill a large pan a quarter full of water. Heat the pan until the water bubbles, then remove the pan from the heat.

5. Put the milk chocolate drops into a heatproof bowl. Wearing oven gloves, carefully put the bowl into the pan.

6. Stir the chocolate with a metal spoon until it has melted. Lift the bowl out of the pan and leave it to cool for three minutes.

Spread the chocolate all the way up the sides.

7. Spread chocolate over the inside of the paper cases using a teaspoon. Put them into a fridge for 20 minutes, until firm.

8. Spoon a little of the soaked fruit into each chocolate case. Fill each case until it is just over half full.

9. Follow steps 4-6 to melt the white chocolate drops in the same way as you melted the milk chocolate drops.

10. Spoon the melted white chocolate into the milk chocolate cases so that it completely covers the fruit.

11. Use the dried fruit from step 2 to decorate the chocolates. Chill them in a fridge for 30 minutes, then peel off the cases.

You could put the fruit cups in a pretty box and give them to someone as a gift.

Little Christmas trees

You could arrange the presents around the trees.

To make 10 trees and 16 presents, you will need:

275g (9½oz) self-raising flour
225g (8oz) soft margarine
4 tablespoons milk
1 level teaspoon of baking powder
225g (8oz) caster sugar
2-3 drops vanilla essence
4 medium eggs
a 25 x 33cm (13 x 10in) roasting tin

For the decorations:
75g (3oz) butter, softened
175g (6oz) icing sugar
2 teaspoons lemon juice
green, pink and yellow
   food colouring
small sweets

Heat the oven to 180°C, 350°F, gas mark 4, before you start.

❄ The cakes need to be stored in an airtight container and eaten within three days.

Wipe oil on top of the paper, too.

Use a wooden spoon to stir the mixture.

1. Draw around the roasting tin on greaseproof paper and cut out the shape. Wipe oil inside the tin, then put the paper into the tin.

2. Sift the flour through a sieve into a large mixing bowl. Add the margarine, milk, baking powder, sugar and vanilla essence.

3. Break the eggs into a small bowl and mix them with a fork. Add them to the large bowl and stir the mixture until it is smooth.

Make trunks for the trees from chocolate bars or biscuits.

Be careful – the cake will be hot.

Use a sieve.

4. Spoon the mixture into the tin and smooth the top. Bake it for 40-45 minutes, until the middle is springy when you press it.

5. After five minutes, lift the cake out of the tin and leave it to cool. For the icing, put the butter into a bowl and stir it until it is creamy.

6. Add the icing sugar, a little at a time, stirring it in each time. Stir in the lemon juice. Put three quarters of the icing in a different bowl.

To make the colour stronger, add more colouring, a drop at a time.

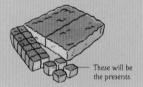

These will be the presents.

Press on sweets to decorate.

7. Mix a few drops of green food colouring into the icing. Divide the rest of the icing in half. Add a different colour to each half and mix it in.

8. Cut a strip 7cm (3in) wide from one end of the cake. Cut it into 16 small squares. Then, cut the cake in half along its length.

9. Cut each strip into five triangles, for the trees. Ice them using the green icing. Then, ice the presents with the other colours of icing.

Mini florentines

To make about 18 mini florentines, you will need:

18 glacé cherries
18 unsalted halved walnuts or pecan nuts*
75g (3oz) plain chocolate drops
75g (3oz) white chocolate drops
a baking tray lined with baking parchment

❄ Keep the florentines in an airtight container, in a fridge, and eat them within four days.

* Don't give these to anyone
who is allergic to nuts.

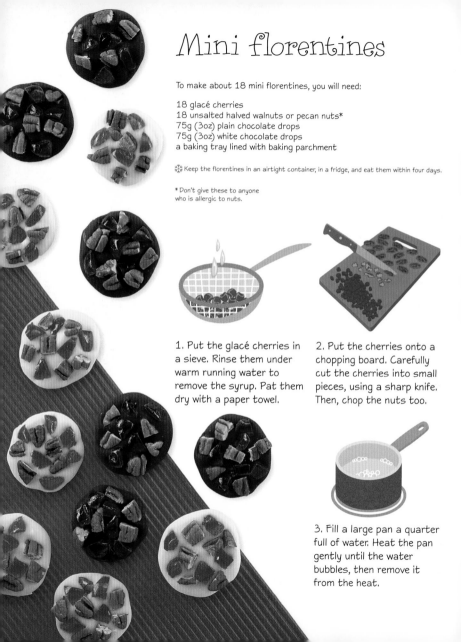

1. Put the glacé cherries in a sieve. Rinse them under warm running water to remove the syrup. Pat them dry with a paper towel.

2. Put the cherries onto a chopping board. Carefully cut the cherries into small pieces, using a sharp knife. Then, chop the nuts too.

3. Fill a large pan a quarter full of water. Heat the pan gently until the water bubbles, then remove it from the heat.

4. Put the plain chocolate drops into a heatproof bowl. Then, wearing oven gloves, carefully put the bowl into the pan.

5. Stir the chocolate with a metal spoon until it has melted. Wearing oven gloves, carefully lift the bowl out of the pan.

6. Spoon a teaspoon of melted chocolate onto the baking parchment. Make it into a neat circle, using the back of the spoon.

7. Gently press pieces of cherry and nut into the chocolate. Make more circles of chocolate and decorate them.

8. Follow steps 3-5 to melt the white chocolate drops. Make more circles with the white chocolate. Then, decorate them, too.

9. Put the florentines in a fridge for half an hour. Then, when the chocolates have hardened, carefully peel them off the paper.

Christmas mice

To make about eight large mice, five medium
mice and three baby mice, you will need:
250g (9oz) icing sugar
200g (8oz) tin of condensed milk
175g (7oz) desiccated coconut
red food colouring
sweets for ears
silver cake-decorating balls
liquorice 'bootlaces'

❄ Keep the mice in an airtight container
and eat them within ten days.

1. Sift the icing sugar
through a sieve into a large
bowl. Add the condensed
milk and the coconut, then
stir everything together.

2. Put the mixture into two
bowls. Mix a few drops of red
food colouring into each bowl.
Then, add a little more
colouring to one of the bowls.

More colouring will
make the mixture a
stronger pink.

For baby mice,
use a teaspoon
for the body.

3. Dip a clean tablespoon into some warm water and let it drip a little. Then, lift a spoonful of the mixture from one of the bowls.

4. Pat the top of the spoonful to make it smooth. Then, turn it over onto a piece of plastic foodwrap and lift off the spoon.

You can use tiny sweets if you don't have any silver balls.

5. Pinch a nose at the thinner end of the spoon shape. Then, add sweets for the mouse's ears and silver balls for eyes.

Use a dessertspoon for a medium mouse.

6. Push a piece of liquorice under the shape, for a tail. Make lots more mice from the mixture and leave them to harden on a plate.

Snowball truffles

To make about 15 truffles, you will need:

175g (6oz) white chocolate drops
25g (1oz) unsalted butter
50g (2oz) plain sponge cake
4 tablespoons desiccated coconut
small paper cases

❄ Keep the truffles in a fridge, in an airtight
container, and eat them within five days.

1. Fill a large pan a
quarter full of water and
heat it until the water
bubbles. Then, remove
the pan from the heat.

2. Put the chocolate drops
and the butter into a
heatproof bowl. Wearing
oven gloves, carefully put
the bowl into the pan.

Keep stirring until
everything has
melted.

3. After two minutes, stir
the chocolate and butter
until they melt. Wearing
oven gloves, carefully lift
the bowl out of the water.

4. Crumble the cake into
fine crumbs. Add the
crumbs to the chocolate
mixture and stir everything
well with a wooden spoon.

You could put
the truffles in a gift
box and give them to
someone for Christmas.

5. Spread the coconut onto
a plate. Scoop up some of
the chocolate mixture with
a teaspoon and put it into
the coconut.

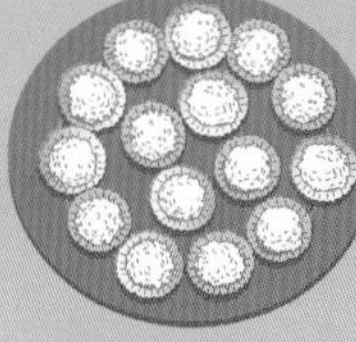

6. Using your fingers, roll
the chocolate mixture in
the coconut to make a
ball. When it is covered,
put it into a paper case.

7. Make more truffles with
the rest of the mixture.
Then, put them onto a
plate and put them in the
fridge to chill for one hour.

21

Chocolate fudge

To make about 36 squares, you will need:

75g (3oz) full-fat cream cheese
350g (12oz) icing sugar
1 level tablespoon of cocoa powder
75g (3oz) plain chocolate drops
40g (1½oz) butter
a shallow 15cm (6in) square cake tin

❄ Keep the fudge in an airtight container
in a fridge, and eat it within a week.

Use a pencil to draw around the tin.

1. Lay the cake tin on a
sheet of greaseproof paper
and draw around it. Then,
cut out the square, just
inside the line.

2. Use a paper towel to
wipe cooking oil onto the
sides and bottom of the
tin. Press in the paper and
wipe the top with oil.

3. Put the cream cheese
into a bowl. Sift the icing
sugar and cocoa through a
sieve into the bowl, too. Mix
everything together well.

4. Melt the chocolate and butter as in steps 1-3 on page 20. Then, stir in a tablespoon of the cream cheese mixture.

5. Pour the chocolate into the cheese mixture. Stir everything together with a spoon, until the mixture is smooth and creamy.

6. Carefully spoon the fudge into the tin, and push it into the corners. You may need to use your fingers to do this.

7. Smooth the top of the fudge with the back of a spoon. Put the tin in a fridge for two hours, or until the fudge is firm.

8. Loosen the edges of the fudge with a blunt knife. Then, turn it out onto a board and remove the greaseproof paper.

9. Cut the fudge into 36 squares. Put the fudge in an airtight container and chill it in a fridge for two more hours.

Snow-covered crispies

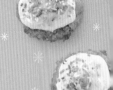

To make about 20 crispies, you will need:

100g (4oz) soft margarine
50g (2oz) butter, softened
50g (2oz) light soft brown sugar
1 egg
1 teaspoon of vanilla essence
125g (5oz) self-raising flour
50g (2oz) corn flakes
200g (7oz) white chocolate drops
sugar sprinkles

Before you start, wipe two
baking trays with cooking oil.
Cut a large piece of greaseproof
paper and put it on a chopping
board, too.
Heat your oven to 190°C,
375°F, gas mark 5.

❄ These crispies are best eaten on the day you make them.

Stir the
mixture
hard.

1. Put the margarine and
butter into a bowl and stir
them until they are creamy.
Add the sugar and stir the
mixture until it is fluffy.

2. Break the egg into a
cup and add the vanilla
essence. Stir the mixture
with a fork, then pour half
of it into the bowl.

Use a
sieve.

3. Stir in the egg mixture.
Then, add the rest and
stir that in, too. Sift the
flour into the bowl, then
stir everything well.

4. Crush the corn flakes
a little with your fingers
and put them onto a plate.
Scoop up a teaspoon of the
mixture and put it on top.

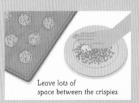

Leave lots of
space between the crispies.

5. Roll the mixture in the
corn flakes to cover it.
Then, put it on a greased
baking tray and make more
crispies in the same way.

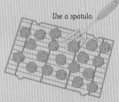

Use a spatula.

6. Bake the crispies for
12-14 minutes. Leave
them on the trays for two
minutes, then lift them
onto a wire rack to cool.

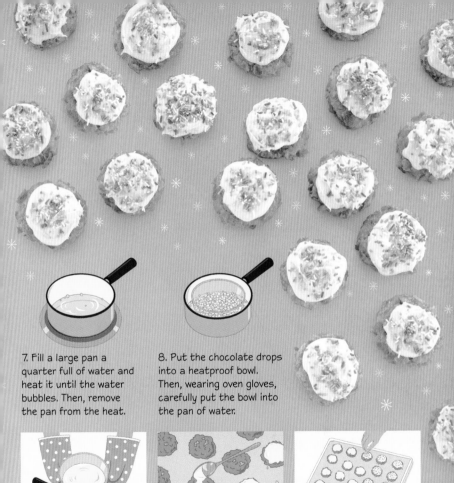

7. Fill a large pan a quarter full of water and heat it until the water bubbles. Then, remove the pan from the heat.

8. Put the chocolate drops into a heatproof bowl. Then, wearing oven gloves, carefully put the bowl into the pan of water.

Wear oven gloves.

9. After two minutes, stir the chocolate drops with a metal spoon until they have melted. Carefully lift the bowl out of the water.

10. Put the crispies onto the chopping board. Then, spread a teaspoon of the melted chocolate over each crispy.

11. Sprinkle sugar sprinkles on the crispies. Put them in the fridge for 20 minutes, for the chocolate to set, or eat them straightaway.

Christmas fairy castle cake

For a cake which will serve 8-10 people, you will need:

175g (6oz) soft margarine
175g (6oz) caster sugar
3 tablespoons milk
1 teaspoon of vanilla essence
200g (7oz) self-raising flour
3 medium eggs
a shallow 18 x 28cm (7 x 11in) cake tin

For the decorations:
225g (8oz) icing sugar
3 tablespoons warm water
1 drop of pink food colouring
writing icing
small sweets

Heat your oven to 180°C, 350°F, gas mark 4, before you start.

❄ Keep the cake in an airtight container or cover it in plastic foodwrap, and eat it within three days.

Use a pencil.

1. Lay the cake tin on a sheet of greaseproof paper and draw around it. Then, cut out the shape, just inside the line.

2. Use a paper towel to wipe some cooking oil on the bottom and sides of the tin. Press in the paper and wipe the top with oil.

3. Put the margarine and sugar into a large bowl. Mix the milk and vanilla essence together and pour them in. Then, sift the flour in, too.

Use a wooden spoon.

4. Break the eggs into a mug and mix them with a fork. Add them to the bowl and stir the mixture until it is smooth and creamy.

Be careful – the cake will be hot.

5. Spoon the mixture into the tin and smooth the top. Bake it for 30-35 minutes, until the middle is springy when you press it.

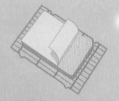

6. After five minutes, run a blunt knife around the cake. Turn it onto a wire rack and peel off the paper, then leave the cake to cool.

Put the strips on the board like this, to make three towers.

7. Put the cake on a board. Cut it into three strips and cut one strip in half. Move a long strip and the short strips onto another board.

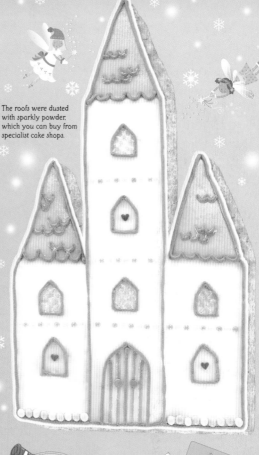

The roofs were dusted with sparkly powder, which you can buy from specialist cake shops.

8. Cut the last strip into three equal pieces. Then, cut the pieces into tall triangles, for roofs. Put them on top of the towers.

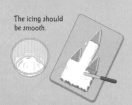

The icing should be smooth.

9. Sift 150g (5oz) of icing sugar into a bowl. Stir in two tablespoons of water, a little at a time, and spread the icing on the towers.

10. Mix the rest of the icing sugar with a drop of pink food colouring and one tablespoon of water. Spread it over the roofs.

11. Use writing icing to draw windows and a door on the castle. Add lines and dots of writing icing, then press on sweets.

Tiny Christmas cookies

To make about 65 tiny cookies, you will need:

50g (2oz) butter, softened
25g (1oz) icing sugar
quarter of a teaspoon of red food colouring
1 teaspoon of milk
quarter of a teaspoon of vanilla essence
75g (3oz) plain flour
little star and heart cutters

Before you start, wipe two baking trays with cooking oil.
Heat your oven to 180°C, 350°F, gas mark 4.

❄ Keep the cookies in an airtight container and eat them within a week.

1. Put the butter into a bowl and stir it until it is creamy. Sift the icing sugar into the bowl and stir it in until the mixture is smooth.

2. Add the food colouring to the mixture and stir it in until the mixture is pink. Then, add the milk and the vanilla essence.

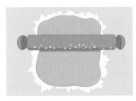

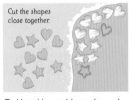

Cut the shapes close together.

3. Sift the flour through a sieve into the bowl and stir everything together. Then, use your hands to squeeze the mixture into a dough.

4. Dust a rolling pin and a clean work surface with flour. Roll out the dough until it is slightly thinner than your little finger.

5. Use the cutters to cut lots of shapes from the dough. Then, use a spatula to lift the shapes onto the baking trays.

6. Squeeze the scraps of dough together to make a ball. Roll out the dough again and cut more shapes. Put them onto the trays.

7. Make patterns on some of the cookies by pushing the end of a cocktail stick into them. Don't worry if it goes all the way through.

Wear oven gloves.

8. Bake the cookies for six to eight minutes. Then, take them out of the oven and leave them on the trays until they are cool.

Some of these cookies were dusted with icing sugar when they were cool.

You could put some cookies into a gift box to give as a present.

Shortbread

To make eight pieces, you will need:

150g (5oz) plain flour
25g (1oz) rice flour or ground rice
100g (4oz) butter, refrigerated, cut into chunks
50g (2oz) caster sugar
a 20cm (8in) shallow round tin

Heat the oven to 150°C, 300°F, gas mark 2, before you start.

❋ Keep the shortbread in an airtight container
and eat it within three days.

1. Rub some butter onto a paper towel, then use it to grease the bottom and sides of the tin. Make sure it is all greased.

2. Sift the flour and rice flour or ground rice through a sieve into a large bowl. Then, add the butter to the bowl, too.

3. Mix in the butter so that it is coated in flour. Then, use your fingers to rub the butter into the flour, until it is like fine breadcrumbs.

Press the mixture against the side of the bowl.

4. Stir in the sugar with a wooden spoon. Hold the bowl with one hand and use your other hand to squeeze the mixture into a ball.

5. Press the mixture into the tin with your fingers. Then, use the back of a spoon to smooth the top and make it level.

6. Use a fork to press patterns and make holes around the edge. Then, cut the shortbread into eight pieces, using a blunt knife.

7. Bake the shortbread for 30 minutes, until it is golden. Leave it in the tin for 10 minutes, then put it onto a wire rack to cool.

Jewelled muffins

To make 12 muffins, you will need:

150ml (¼ pint) milk
65g (2½oz) plain chocolate drops
150g (5oz) caster sugar
65g (2½oz) butter, softened
1 medium egg
150g (5oz) self-raising flour
paper muffin cases
a 12-hole baking or muffin tray

For decorating:
75g (3oz) butter, softened
175g (6oz) icing sugar, sifted
a few drops of vanilla essence
2 teaspoons milk
small sweets and sugar sprinkles

Before you start, put 12 paper muffin cases into the baking tray.
Heat your oven to 190°C, 375°F, gas mark 5, too.

❄ Keep the muffins in an airtight container and eat them within two days.

Keep stirring so that the
mixture does not stick.

1. Put the milk, chocolate drops and 50g (2oz) of the caster sugar into a small pan. Then, gently heat the pan on a low heat.

2. When the chocolate has melted, and the sugar has dissolved, take the pan off the heat. Then, leave the mixture to cool.

3. Put the butter into a large bowl and stir until it is creamy. Add the rest of the sugar and stir the mixture until it is fluffy.

4. Break the egg into a mug and stir it with a fork. Add half of the egg to the bowl and stir it in, then add the rest and stir that in, too.

5. Sift half of the flour through a sieve into the bowl. Pour in half of the chocolate mixture and stir it in with a wooden spoon.

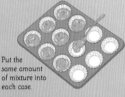

Put the same amount of mixture into each case.

Wear oven gloves.

Stir the mixture hard.

6. Sift in the remaining flour and add the rest of the chocolate mixture. Mix everything well and spoon the mixture into the cases.

7. Bake the muffins for 15 minutes, then take them out of the oven. After five minutes, put them onto a wire rack to cool.

8. For the icing, put the butter into a large bowl and stir it until it is creamy. Add some of the icing sugar and stir it in.

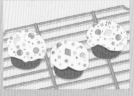

9. Add the rest of the sugar, a little at a time, stirring it in well. Then, add the vanilla essence and milk, and stir them in.

10. Peel the paper cases off the muffins. Use a blunt knife to spread icing on top of them, then press on sweets to decorate.

Snow cloud meringues

To make about 30 meringues,
you will need:

2 eggs, at room temperature
100g (4oz) caster sugar
sugar sprinkles

Heat your oven to 110°C, 225°F,
gas mark ¼, before you start.

❄ Keep the meringues in an airtight
container and eat them within a week.

Cut inside the lines.

1. Draw around a baking
tray on baking parchment.
Cut out the shape and put
it in the tray. Then, do the
same with another tray.

You could use a yolk to make painted
biscuits (see pages 44-45).

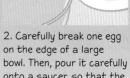

2. Carefully break one egg
on the edge of a large
bowl. Then, pour it carefully
onto a saucer, so that the
egg yolk doesn't break.

3. Hold an egg cup over
the yolk and carefully tip
the saucer over the bowl
so that the egg white
dribbles into it.

4. Repeat steps 2-3 with
the other egg so that
both egg whites are in the
bowl. You don't need the
egg yolks.

5. Whisk the egg whites
with a whisk until they are
really thick. They should
form stiff points when you
lift the whisk up.

6. Add a tablespoon of sugar to the egg whites and whisk it in well. Whisk in the rest of the sugar a tablespoon at a time.

7. Scoop up a teaspoon of the meringue mixture. Then, use another teaspoon to push it off onto one of the baking trays.

8. Make more meringues until you have used all the mixture. Then, sprinkle a few sugar sprinkles over each one.

9. Put the meringues into the oven and bake them for 40 minutes. Then, turn off the oven, leaving the meringues inside.

Wear oven gloves.

10. After 15 minutes, carefully lift the baking trays out of the oven. Leave the meringues on the trays to cool.

Peppermint creams

To make about 40 peppermint creams, you will need:

250g (9oz) icing sugar
half the white of a small egg (2½ teaspoons), mixed
  from dried egg white (mix as directed on the packet)
1 teaspoon of peppermint flavouring
2 teaspoons lemon juice
red and green food colouring
small cutters
a baking tray covered
  in plastic foodwrap

❋ Keep the peppermint creams in an airtight
  container and eat them within two weeks.

1. Sift the icing sugar through a sieve into a large bowl. Then, make a small hollow in the middle of the sugar using a spoon.

2. Mix together the egg white, peppermint flavouring and lemon juice in a small bowl. Pour the mixture into the middle of the sugar.

3. Stir everything together using a blunt knife. Squeeze the mixture between your fingers until it is smooth, then cut it into two halves.

4. Put each half into a separate bowl. Add a few drops of red food colouring to one bowl, and a few drops of green to the other.

Add icing sugar if the mixture is sticky.

5. Use your fingers to mix in the red colouring. Wash your hands, then mix the green colouring into the mixture in the other bowl.

Use a sieve.

6. Sprinkle a little icing sugar onto a clean work surface. Sprinkle some onto a rolling pin too, to stop the mixture sticking.

You could put the peppermint creams in boxes to give as gifts.

Cut the shapes close together.

7. Roll out the pink mixture until it is about as thick as your little finger. Then, use small cutters to cut out lots of shapes.

8. Lift the shapes onto the baking tray. Squeeze the scraps into a ball and roll it out. Cut out more shapes and put them onto the tray.

9. Roll out the green mixture and cut out more shapes. Then, leave all the shapes on the tray for an hour, to harden.

Starry jam tart

To make one jam tart, you will need:

350g (12oz) packet shortcrust pastry,
  taken out of the fridge 10 minutes before
  you start.
about 2 tablespoons plain flour
6 rounded tablespoons seedless raspberry
  or strawberry jam

milk for glazing
20cm (8in) fluted flan tin
a small star-shaped cutter

Heat the oven to 200°C, 400°F, gas mark 6, before you start.

❄ Keep the tart in an airtight container and eat it within three days.

You can use any
shape of cutter you
like. Stars and holly
leaves look very
Christmassy.

1. Sprinkle some plain flour over a clean work surface and onto a rolling pin. The flour will stop the pastry from sticking.

2. Cut off a quarter of the pastry. Then, wrap it in some plastic foodwrap and put it to one side until step 6.

Sift a little icing sugar onto a slice of tart and serve it with cream.

The rolling pin cuts off the extra pastry.

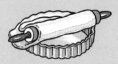

3. Roll out the bigger piece of pastry. Then, turn it a little and roll it again to make a circle about 30cm (12in) across.

4. Put the rolling pin at one side of the pastry. Roll the pastry around it and lift it up. Place the pastry over the tin and unroll it.

5. Dip a finger into some flour and press the pastry into the edges of the tin. Then, roll the rolling pin across the top.

Use a pastry brush.

The pastry will be golden brown.

6. Spoon the jam into the pastry case. Spread it out with the back of a spoon. Roll out the other quarter of the pastry.

7. Using the cutter, cut out about 12 pastry shapes. Brush them with a little milk and place them on top of the jam.

8. Bake the jam tart for about 20 minutes. Wearing oven gloves, take the tart out of the oven. Let the jam cool before serving.

Christmas tree cakes

To make 15 cakes, you will need:

100g (4oz) self-raising flour
2 medium eggs
100g (4oz) soft margarine
100g (4oz) caster sugar
paper cases
two 12-hole baking trays

For decorating:
75g (3oz) butter or margarine, softened
175g (6oz) icing sugar
2 teaspoons lemon juice or a few drops of vanilla essence
small sweets and silver cake-decorating balls.

Heat the oven to 190°C, 375°F, gas mark 5, before you start.

❄ Keep the cakes in an airtight container and eat
them within two days.

1. Sift the flour through a sieve into a large bowl. Break the eggs into a mug and stir them with a fork. Add the eggs to the bowl.

2. Add the margarine and sugar. Then, use a wooden spoon to stir everything together until the mixture is smooth and creamy.

3. Put 15 paper cases into the pans in the baking trays. Then, use a spoon to half-fill each case with the cake mixture.

Leave the cakes to cool.

4. Bake the cakes for 20 minutes. Wear oven gloves to take the cakes out of the oven. After five minutes move them onto a wire rack.

5. For the icing, put the butter or margarine into a large bowl and stir it well using a fork. Carry on until it is really creamy.

6. Add some of the icing sugar and stir it in. Then, add the rest of the icing sugar, a little at a time, stirring it in each time.

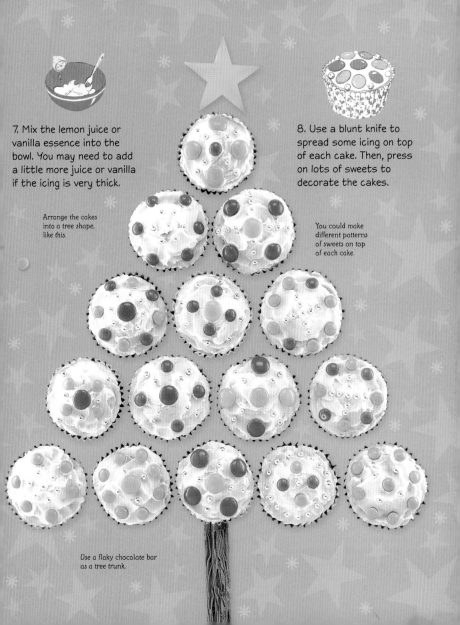

7. Mix the lemon juice or vanilla essence into the bowl. You may need to add a little more juice or vanilla if the icing is very thick.

Arrange the cakes into a tree shape, like this.

8. Use a blunt knife to spread some icing on top of each cake. Then, press on lots of sweets to decorate the cakes.

You could make different patterns of sweets on top of each cake.

Use a flaky chocolate bar as a tree trunk.

Iced gingerbread hearts

To make about 20 biscuits, you will need:

350g (12oz) plain flour
2 teaspoons ground ginger
1 teaspoon bicarbonate of soda
100g (4oz) butter or margarine, cut into chunks
175g (6oz) soft light brown sugar
1 medium egg
4 tablespoons golden syrup
white writing icing
silver cake-decorating balls
or small sweets
a large heart-shaped cutter

Before you start, wipe cooking oil over
two baking trays. Heat the oven
to 190°C, 375°F, gas mark 5, too.

❄ Keep the biscuits in an airtight container
and eat them within three days.

You could wrap some
biscuits in tissue paper
or cellophane twists, to
give as a present.

1. Sift the flour, ground ginger and bicarbonate of soda through a sieve into a large bowl. Add the butter or margarine chunks.

2. Use your fingers to rub the butter or margarine into the flour until it is like fine breadcrumbs. Then, stir in the sugar.

3. Break the egg into a small bowl and add the syrup. Using a fork, stir the mixture well, then add it to the large bowl.

4. Mix everything with a metal spoon to make a dough. Sprinkle flour onto a clean work surface, then put the dough onto it.

Do this until the dough is smooth.

5. Dust flour onto your hands, then stretch the dough by pushing it away from you. Fold the dough in half and repeat.

Sprinkle more flour onto the work surface.

6. Cut the dough in half and sprinkle flour onto a rolling pin. Roll out half the dough until it is a little thinner than your little finger.

7. Use the heart-shaped cutter to cut out lots of hearts. Then, use a spatula to lift the hearts onto the baking trays.

8. Roll out the rest of the dough. Cut out more hearts and put them on the baking trays. Wearing oven gloves, put the trays in the oven.

9. Bake the biscuits for 12-15 minutes, until they are golden brown. Wearing oven gloves, carefully lift the trays from the oven.

10. Leave the biscuits on the trays for about 5 minutes. Then, use a spatula to lift them onto a wire rack and leave them to cool.

11. When the biscuits are cold, draw lines across them with writing icing. Cross some of the lines over each other, like this.

12. Leave the icing for a few minutes, to harden. Then, press cake-decorating balls, or small sweets into the icing, where the lines cross.

Painted biscuits

To make about 15 biscuits, you will need:

50g (2oz) icing sugar
75g (3oz) soft margarine
the yolk from a large egg
2-3 drops of vanilla essence
150g (5oz) plain flour
big cutters

To decorate the biscuits:
an egg yolk
different food colourings

Before you start, wipe cooking over a baking sheet. Heat the oven to 180°C, 350°F, gas mark 4, too.

❄ Keep the biscuits in an airtight container and eat within five days.

Use a wooden spoon.

1. Sift the icing sugar through a sieve into a large bowl. Then, add the margarine and stir the mixture until it is smooth.

2. Add the large egg yolk to the bowl and stir it in well. Then, add the drops of vanilla essence. Stir in the vanilla.

Flatten the dough a little before you wrap it.

3. Sift the flour into the mixture and stir it in with a wooden spoon. Then, use your hands to squeeze the mixture to make a dough.

4. Wrap the dough in plastic foodwrap. Then, put the dough in a freezer while you make the 'paint' to decorate the biscuits.

Use the ideas on these pages to paint patterns on your biscuits.

You could use festive cutters, such as holly leaves and bells.

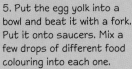

5. Put the egg yolk into a bowl and beat it with a fork. Put it onto saucers. Mix a few drops of different food colouring into each one.

6. Sprinkle flour over a clean work surface and onto a rolling pin. Then, roll out the dough until it is as thin as your little finger.

7. Press out shapes using the cutters. Use a spatula to lift them onto the baking sheet. Squeeze the scraps into a ball.

Use a clean paintbrush to paint the patterns.

8. Roll out the ball and cut out more shapes. Paint patterns on the biscuits. Then, bake the biscuits for 10-12 minutes.

9. Wearing oven gloves, take the biscuits out of the oven. Leave them for five minutes, then lift them onto a wire rack to cool.

Sparkly stars

To make 20 biscuits, you will need:

3 tablespoons caster sugar
4 drops pink food colouring
75g (3oz) butter, softened
1 small lemon
25g (1oz) soft light brown sugar
3 tablespoons clear honey
1 medium egg
175g (6oz) plain flour
medium and small star cutters

Before you start, wipe two
baking trays with cooking oil.
Heat your oven to 180°C,
350°F, gas mark 4 in step 7.

❄ The biscuits need to be stored in an
airtight container and eaten within
five days.

1. Put the caster sugar
into a bowl, then add the
food colouring. Stir the
sugar until it is pink. Then,
spread it on a plate to dry.

Use the fine holes
on the grater.

2. Put the butter into a
large bowl and stir it until
it is creamy. Then, grate
the rind off the lemon and
add the rind to the bowl.

3. Add the brown sugar
and the honey to the bowl.
Then, stir everything
together well until the
mixture is smooth.

4. Carefully break the egg
on the edge of a bowl. Then,
pour the egg carefully onto
a saucer, so that the egg
yolk doesn't break.

Keep the egg white
for later.

5. Put an egg cup over the
yolk. Tip the saucer so that
the egg white dribbles into
a bowl. Then, stir the yolk
into the honey mixture.

The flour will stop the dough from sticking.

6. Use a sieve to sift the flour into the mixture. Stir it in, then squeeze the mixture to make a dough. Wrap it in plastic foodwrap.

7. Chill the dough in a fridge for 30 minutes. While it is chilling, heat your oven. Dust a clean work surface and a rolling pin with flour.

Cut the stars close together.

8. Roll out the dough until it is slightly thinner than your little finger. Then, use the medium cutter to cut out lots of shapes.

9. Use the small cutter to cut a star from the middle of each biscuit. Press the scraps into a ball, roll it out and cut out more stars.

Wear oven gloves.

10. Brush a little egg white over each star and sprinkle pink sugar on top. Then, use a spatula to lift the stars onto the baking trays.

11. Bake the biscuits for 8-10 minutes, and then take them out of the oven. After five minutes, lift them onto a wire rack to cool.

Chocolate swirls

To make about 25 chocolate swirls, you will need:

250g (9oz) icing sugar
half the white of a medium egg (3 teaspoons), mixed
  from dried egg white (mixed as directed on the packet)
1 teaspoon of lemon juice
1 teaspoon of peppermint flavouring
1 tablespoon of cocoa powder
2 teaspoons boiling water
1 teaspoon of vanilla flavouring
a baking tray covered in plastic foodwrap

❄ The swirls need to be kept in an airtight container,
  in a fridge, and eaten within ten days.

Use a sieve.

1. Sift 100g (4oz) of icing
sugar into a large bowl.
Then, make a small hollow
in the middle of the sugar
with a spoon.

2. Mix half of the egg white
with the lemon juice and
peppermint in a small bowl.
Pour the mixture into the
hollow in the sugar.

3. Stir the mixture with a
blunt knife, then squeeze it
with your fingers until it is
smooth. Wrap the mixture
in plastic foodwrap.

4. Sift the cocoa powder into a large bowl. Add the water and vanilla flavouring, then mix everything together well.

5. Add the rest of the egg white and stir it in. Sift the rest of the icing sugar into the bowl. Then, stir the mixture with a blunt knife.

If the mixture is a little dry, add a drop of water.

6. Squeeze the mixture until it is smooth. Wrap it in foodwrap, too. Then, put the two mixtures in a fridge for 10 minutes.

7. Sprinkle a little icing sugar onto a clean work surface and a rolling pin. The icing sugar stops the mixture from sticking.

8. Roll out the white mixture into a rectangle 20cm x 15cm (8in x 6in). Then, do the same with the chocolate mixture.

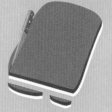

9. Put the chocolate rectangle on top of the white one. Then, trim the edges with a knife to make them straight.

Roll the rectangle from one of the long edges.

10. Tightly roll the rectangle into a sausage. Then, wrap it in foodwrap and put it in a fridge for about 10 minutes.

11. Take off the foodwrap. Then, use a sharp knife to carefully cut the sausage into slices about as thick as your little finger.

12. Put the swirls onto the foodwrap-covered baking tray. Then, leave the swirls in a cool, dry place to harden overnight.

Jolly jam biscuits

To make about 20 biscuits, you will need:

100g (4oz) butter, softened
1 teaspoon of vanilla essence
50g (2oz) icing sugar
100g (4oz) plain flour
25g (1oz) cornflour
25g (1oz) desiccated coconut
about 2 tablespoons of seedless raspberry or
  strawberry jam

Before you start, wipe two baking trays with cooking oil.
Heat your oven to 180°C, 350°F, gas mark 4.

❄️ Keep the biscuits in an airtight container
   and eat them within five days.

1. Put the butter into a
large bowl and stir it until
it is creamy. Then, add
the vanilla essence and
stir it in.

2. Sift the icing sugar
through a sieve into the
bowl. Then, stir the
mixture well until it is
smooth and creamy.

3. Sift the flour and the
cornflour into the bowl.
Then, add the coconut
and stir everything well
to make a soft dough.

4. Rub some flour on your
hands. Then, scoop up a
little of the dough with
a teaspoon and roll it into
a smooth ball.

5. Make more balls and
put them on the greased
baking trays. Leave spaces
between the balls, because
they spread as they cook.

6. Push your little finger into the middle of each ball, to make a hollow. Push it in up to the first knuckle, like this.

Wear oven gloves.

7. Bake the biscuits for 12-14 minutes. Carefully lift them out of the oven, then leave them to cool on the trays.

8. When the biscuits have cooled, sift a little icing sugar over them. Then, use a teaspoon to fill the holes with jam.

Crinkly Christmas pies

To make 12 pies, you will need:

4 eating apples
3 tablespoons orange juice
50g (2oz) dried cranberries or sultanas
2 teaspoons caster sugar
half a teaspoon of ground cinnamon
100g (4oz) filo pastry (about 6 sheets)
50g (2oz) butter
icing sugar for dusting
a baking tray with shallow pans or 12-hole muffin tin

Heat the oven to 190°C, 375°F, gas mark 5, before you start.

❄ Keep the pies in an airtight container and eat them within five days.

You may need to ask someone to help you.

Put the lid back on after you've stirred the apples.

Stir the mixture often.

1. Carefully peel the apples with a vegetable peeler. Cut them into quarters and cut out the cores. Then, cut the quarters into small pieces.

2. Put the pieces into a pan and add the juice. Cover the pan with a lid. Heat the pan on a very low heat for 20 minutes, stirring often.

3. Stir in the dried fruit, caster sugar and cinnamon. Cook the mixture for about five minutes, then take it off the heat.

Use a pastry brush.

4. Unwrap the pastry sheets. Then, keeping the sheets together, cut them into six pieces, like this. Cover them with foodwrap.

5. Put the butter into a small pan and melt it over a low heat. Brush a little butter over one of the pastry squares.

6. Gently press the square into a hole in the tray, so that the buttered side faces up. Then, brush butter onto another square.

Overlap the pastry sheets so that they look like a star.

7. Put the second square on top of the first one, so the corners overlap a little. Add a third square, too. Fill all the holes in this way.

Eat the pies warm or cold.

Wear oven gloves.

Heat the mixture until it bubbles slightly.

Use a small sieve if you have one.

8. Bake the pastry cases on the middle shelf of the oven for 10 minutes. Take them out, then leave them to cool for five minutes.

9. Take the cases out of the tray and put them onto a large plate. Heat the apple mixture again for about two minutes.

10. Spoon the apple mixture into the pastry cases, so that they are almost full. Sift a little icing sugar over the pies.

Frosty fudge

To make about 50 pieces of fudge, you will need:

350g (12oz) icing sugar
75g (3oz) unsalted butter
4 teaspoons milk
half a teaspoon of vanilla essence
75g (3oz) pink and white marshmallows
2 tablespoons sugar sprinkles
a shallow 18cm (7in) square tin

❄ Keep the fudge in a fridge, in an airtight container, and eat it within a week.

Put the bowl to one side until step 6.

1. Lay the tin on a piece of greaseproof paper. Draw around it with a pencil, then cut out the square, just inside the line.

2. Use a paper towel to wipe cooking oil onto the sides and bottom of the tin. Press in the paper square and wipe it with oil.

3. Sift the icing sugar through a sieve into a large bowl. Then, make a small hollow in the middle of the sugar with a spoon.

Use a pair of kitchen scissors.

4. Put the butter, milk and vanilla essence into a small pan. Then, cut the marshmallows in half and add them to the pan.

5. Gently heat the pan. Stir the mixture every now and then with a wooden spoon, until everything has melted.

6. Pour the mixture into the hollow in the middle of the sugar. Then, quickly stir everything together, until the mixture is smooth.

Smooth the top with the back of a spoon.

7. Pour the fudge into the tin and push it into the corners. Smooth the top, then sprinkle the sugar sprinkles over the fudge.

Press them in firmly.

8. Use your fingers to press the sugar sprinkles into the fudge. When the fudge is cool, chill it in a fridge for two hours.

9. Loosen the edges of the fudge with a blunt knife. Then, carefully turn it out onto a board and remove the greaseproof paper.

Try not to knock off the sugar sprinkles.

10. Turn the fudge over and cut it into small squares. Put the fudge in an airtight container and chill it in the fridge for two more hours.

You could put the fudge into a cellophane bag and give it to someone as a present.

Chocolate truffles

To make about 10 truffles, you will need:

100g (4oz) milk chocolate drops
25g (1oz) butter
25g (1oz) icing sugar
50g (2oz) plain sponge cake, crumbled into fine crumbs
4 tablespoons chocolate sugar strands
small paper cases

❄ Keep the truffles in an airtight container, in a
fridge and eat them within five days.

You could put the truffles
in boxes lined with tissue
paper, to give as presents.

1. Fill a large pan a quarter full of water and heat it until the water bubbles. Then, remove the pan from the heat.

2. Put the chocolate drops and butter into a heatproof bowl. Wearing oven gloves, carefully put the bowl into the pan.

3. Stir the chocolate and butter with a metal spoon until they have melted. Then, wearing oven gloves, carefully lift the bowl out of the pan.

4. Sift the icing sugar through a sieve into the chocolate. Add the cake crumbs and stir until everything is mixed well.

5. Leave the chocolate mixture to cool in the bowl. While the mixture cools, spread the chocolate strands onto a plate.

6. When the chocolate mixture is firm and thick, scoop up a little with a teaspoon and put it into the chocolate strands.

7. Using your fingers, gently roll the spoonful into a ball around the plate, until it is covered with strands. Put it into a paper case.

8. Make lots more truffles in the same way. Put all the truffles onto a plate, then put them in a fridge to chill for 30 minutes.

Snowmen and presents

To make lots of snowmen
and presents, you will need:

250g (9oz) 'white'
 marzipan, cut from a block*
green, red and yellow
 food colouring
toothpicks

* Marzipan contains
ground nuts, so don't
give it to anyone who is
allergic to nuts.

❄ The marzipan needs to
be stored in an airtight
container and eaten
within three weeks.

Colouring marzipan

Add a little icing sugar
if the marzipan gets
too sticky.

1. Unwrap the marzipan
and put it onto a plate.
Then, cut it into four pieces
and put each piece into a
small bowl.

2. Add a drop of green food
colouring to one of the
bowls. Mix it in with your
fingers until the marzipan
is evenly coloured.

3. Add red colouring to one
bowl and yellow to another,
then mix in the colours.
Leave the last piece of
marzipan 'white'.

A snowman

Put the marzipan
balls onto a plate.

Press the ball with
your thumb.

Cross the ends
of the scarf.

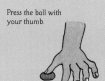

1. Roll a piece of 'white'
marzipan into a ball. Then,
make a smaller ball. Press
the smaller ball on top of
the larger one, for a head.

2. Roll a small ball of red
marzipan. Press it to make
a flat circle, then put it on
the snowman's head. Add a
tiny red ball on top.

3. Roll a thin sausage from
red marzipan. Wrap it
around the snowman for a
scarf. Use a toothpick to
make the snowman's face.

You could arrange your snowmen and presents on top of an iced Christmas cake.

A present

Make presents from the other colours, too.

1. Roll a small ball from red marzipan and put it on a clean work surface. Gently press the flat side of a knife down on the ball.

2. Turn the ball on its side and press it with the knife again. Keep on turning and pressing the marzipan until the ball becomes a cube.

3. Roll long, thin sausages from green marzipan. Press two onto the cube, in a cross. Then, add two loops in the middle for a bow.

Christmas crunchies

To make about 15 crunchies, you will need:

25g (1oz) glacé cherries
25g (1oz) rich tea or other plain biscuits
25g (1oz) white marshmallows
100g (4oz) white chocolate drops
25g (1oz) unsalted butter
15 dried cranberries
small paper cases

❄ Keep the crunchies in an airtight container,
in a fridge, and eat them within a week.

1. Cut the cherries into tiny pieces and put them into a large bowl. Then, break the biscuits into lots of little pieces and add them, too.

2. Cut the marshmallows into small pieces, using a pair of kitchen scissors. Add them to the bowl and mix everything together.

3. Fill a large pan a quarter full of water and heat it until the water bubbles. Then, remove the pan from the heat.

4. Put the chocolate drops and the butter into a heatproof bowl. Wearing oven gloves, carefully put the bowl into the pan.

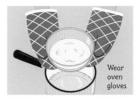

Wear oven gloves.

5. After two minutes, stir the mixture with a metal spoon. When everything has melted, carefully lift the bowl out of the pan.

6. Spoon the chocolate and butter mixture into the large bowl. Then, mix everything well with a wooden spoon.

7. Use a teaspoon to scoop up some of the mixture. Shape the mixture into a ball with your fingers and put it into a paper case.

8. Make more balls in the same way, until you have used all the mixture. Then, press a dried cranberry onto the top of each one.

9. Put all the crunchies onto a large plate. Then, put the plate in a fridge and leave them to chill for two hours.

Cool coconut ice

To make 36 squares, you will need:

2 egg whites, mixed from dried egg white
(mix as directed on the packet)
450g (1lb) icing sugar, sifted
175g (6oz) desiccated coconut
4 teaspoons water
green food colouring
a shallow 18cm (7in) square cake tin
greaseproof paper

❄ Keep the coconut ice in an airtight container
and eat it within 10 days.

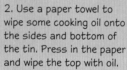

1. Lay the cake tin on a
piece of greaseproof paper
and draw around it using a
pencil. Then, cut out the
square, just inside the line.

2. Use a paper towel to
wipe some cooking oil onto
the sides and bottom of
the tin. Press in the paper
and wipe the top with oil.

3. Put the egg whites into
a large bowl. Stir them
quickly with a fork for
about a minute, until they
are frothy.

To make pink and
white coconut ice, use
red food colouring
instead of green.

4. Sift two tablespoons of icing sugar into the bowl and stir it in. Sift in the rest of the sugar a little a time, stirring it in each time.

5. Add the coconut and water and mix everything well. Spoon half of the mixture into the tin. Use your fingers to press it in.

6. Add a few drops of green food colouring to the rest of the mixture. Stir the mixture with a metal spoon until it is evenly coloured.

Smooth the top with the back of a spoon.

 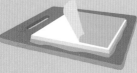 

7. Spoon the green mixture on top of the white layer. Smooth the top a little, then leave the tin in a cool place overnight.

8. Use a blunt knife to loosen the edges of the coconut ice. Then, turn it out onto a chopping board and remove the paper.

9. Carefully cut the coconut ice into 36 squares using a sharp knife. Then, leave the pieces on the board for two hours, to harden.

Marzipan canes

To make four canes, you will need:

90g (3½oz) 'white' marzipan*, cut from a block
red food colouring

❄ Keep the canes in an airtight container and eat them within three weeks.

* Marzipan contains ground nuts, so don't give the canes to anyone who is allergic to nuts.

The sticks should be twice as long as your middle finger.

1. Cut the marzipan into three pieces the same size. Then, cut two of the pieces in half and roll them into sticks.

Add pink food colouring in step 2 to make a cane like the one below.

2. Put the remaining piece of marzipan into a small bowl. Add three drops of red food colouring and mix it in with your fingers.

3. Cut the red marzipan into four pieces. Roll each piece into a thin stick, about three times as long as your middle finger.

Hold this end as you wind.

4. Starting at one end, wind a red stick around a white one, like this. Do this with all the sticks, to make three more stripy sticks.

5. Roll the sticks on a clean work surface to make them smooth. Then, bend the end of each one into a curve, to make a cane.

Managing editor: Fiona Watt • Photographic manipulation: John Russell
First published in 2006 by Usborne Publishing Ltd., Usborne House, 83-85 Saffron Hill, London, EC1N 8RT, England. www.usborne.com